DOROTHEA LANGE

A Life in Pictures

Other titles in the **People to Know Today** series:

Lance Armstrong
Cycling, Surviving, Inspiring Hope
ISBN-13: 978-0-7660-2694-0
ISBN-10:   0-7660-2694-9

Bill Gates
Computer Mogul and Philanthropist
ISBN-13: 978-0-7660-2693-3
ISBN-10:   0-7660-2693-0

George W. Bush
President in a Turbulent World
ISBN-13: 978-0-7660-2628-5
ISBN-10:   0-7660-2628-0

Dorothea Lange
A Life in Pictures
ISBN-13: 978-0-7660-2697-1
ISBN-10:   0-7660-2697-3

Laura Bush
Portrait of a First Lady
ISBN-13: 978-0-7660-2629-2
ISBN-10:   0-7660-2629-9

J. K. Rowling
Author of *Harry Potter*
ISBN-13: 978-0-7660-1850-1
ISBN-10:   0-7660-1850-4

Walt Disney
Genius of Entertainment
ISBN-13: 978-0-7660-2624-7
ISBN-10:   0-7660-2624-8

Arnold Schwarzenegger
From Superstar to Governor
ISBN-13: 978-0-7660-2625-4
ISBN-10:   0-7660-2625-6

Robert Frost
The Life of America's Poet
ISBN-13: 978-0-7660-2627-8
ISBN-10:   0-7660-2627-2

Sam Walton
Business Genius of Wal-Mart
ISBN-13: 978-0-7660-2692-6
ISBN-10:   0-7660-2692-2

DOROTHEA LANGE

A Life in Pictures

Laura Baskes Litwin

Enslow Publishers, Inc.
40 Industrial Road
Box 398
Berkeley Heights, NJ 07922
USA

http://www.enslow.com

Library of Congress Cataloging-in-Publication Data

Litwin, Laura Baskes.
    Dorothea Lange : a life in pictures / Laura Baskes Litwin.
        p. cm. — (People to know today)
    Includes bibliographical references and index
    ISBN-13: 978-0-7660-2697-1
    ISBN-10: 0-7660-2697-3
    1. Lange, Dorothea—Juvenile literature. 2. Women photographers—United States—
Biography—Juvenile literature. 3. Photographers—United States—Biography—Juvenile literature.
I. Title.
TR140.L3L58 2007
770.92—dc22
[B]   2006036507

Printed in the United States of America

10 9 8 7 6 5 4 3 2 1

To Our Readers: We have done our best to make sure all Internet addresses in this book were active
and appropriate when we went to press. However, the author and publisher have no control over
and assume no liability for the material available on those Internet sites or on other Web sites they
may link to. Any comments or suggestions can be sent by e-mail to comments@enslow.com or to
the address on the back cover.

Photos and Illustrations: AP/Wide World Photos, p. 107; Courtesy Peter Brown and Harris
Gallery, Houston, p. 109; Nicole DiMella/Enslow Publishers, Inc., p. 14; Dorothea Lange,
Oakland Museum of California, Gift of Paul S. Taylor, pp. 18, 38, 40, 42, 44, 48, 52, 60,
79, 85, 89, 96, 101, 102; Library of Congress, pp. 3, 6, 9, 11, 15, 24, 28, 50, 55, 64, 66,
68, 69, 74; National Archives, p. 76; New York Public Library, pp. 31, 35; Northern Arizona
University, Cline Library, Special Collections and Archives, Bill Belknap Collection, p. 92.

Cover Illustration: Dorothea Lange, Oakland Museum of California, Gift of Paul S. Taylor.

CONTENTS

Dorothea Lange

1

HEARTBREAK IN THE HEARTLAND

It was the end of a very long day. A day that had begun at dawn with a hastily gobbled breakfast and continued uninterrupted with no break even for lunch. It was a Sunday, the usual day of rest, but no one who worked here took much stock in rest.

For Dorothea Lange, this was a new job. A job she had been promised only for a month. In thirty days, Lange understood she had to prove her worth or be let go. She had been hired under false pretenses. Her supervisor had added her name to the payroll as a clerk typist. Lange was not a particularly good typist. What she was, in fact, was a very good photographer.

Lange really needed the job. This was April 1935, and the country was in the midst of the worst economic depression in its history. One of every four Americans was out of work. Lange felt the pressures of having to quickly convince her superiors she was someone they wanted to keep.

Dorothea Lange was hired to take pictures for an economist named Paul Taylor who was doing a study of workers in California. She had to be called a typist for the payroll accounts because at that time no one had ever heard of hiring photographers to do this kind of work.

The particular workers the economist was interested in studying were called migrant workers. For close to a hundred years, migrant workers in California were typically Mexican, Chinese, and Filipino immigrants who had come to the United States seeking jobs. They stayed to pick grapes, peas, almonds, lettuce, and other crops that grew so easily in the mild climate.

But California proved not to be the promised land of the agricultural migrants' dreams. Their living and working conditions were appalling. Paul Taylor and his staff planned to document the workers' circumstances. A professor at the University of California at Berkeley, Taylor had performed many studies before, but now, for the first time, Dorothea Lange's photographs would help to reinforce his research.

Taylor wanted Lange to take pictures of something else as well—a new breed of migrant worker suddenly arriving in California. Although traditional migrants were single men, these new outsiders were crossing the state's border as whole families traveling together. At the outset, no one was entirely certain who these people were. They appeared to be farmers. Many small farmers were suffering due to the wrecked economy of the Great Depression, but why had they left their farms? Even in the worst of times, a farmer could grow enough at least to feed his family.

Skid Row—a portrait photograph taken by Dorothea Lange on Howard Street in San Francisco in 1937.

The answer was plain and horrifying—their farms had blown away. After years of extreme drought, the topsoil in their fields had dried up and simply blew away. Thunderous black clouds of dust traveling at speeds of up to sixty miles an hour darkened the skies. The dust made it impossible to farm and difficult even to breathe.

During her first few days at work, Dorothea Lange did not encounter any of these new migrants, but at dusk on this particular Sunday, while waiting to put gas in her car, she noticed a distinctive family ahead of her at the pump. Their battered old car was laden down with trunks, bedding, hand tools, and cast-iron cooking pots. Their license plate said Oklahoma: they had come a long way. Lange approached the family with her camera in hand. As was always her way, she spoke first, gently and with respect, asking permission before taking a single picture. She observed,

> *They looked very woebegone to me . . . I asked which way were they going, were they looking for work? And they said, 'We've been blown out.' I questioned what that meant, and then they told me about the dust storm. They were the first arrivals that I saw. These were the people who got up that day quick and left. They saw they had no crop back there. They had to get out.*[1]

Dorothea Lange took photographs of this family and many others like them in the months that

A Lange photo of two men walking toward Los Angeles, California.

followed. She so impressed Paul Taylor with her gifts as a photographer and a human being that he not only kept her on the job, he married her.

When she was still in her teens, Lange announced out of the blue that she wanted to be a photographer. For a woman in the early part of the last century, this was neither a customary nor an easy career choice, but from the time she was a little girl, Lange had proven she was up to the challenge.

2

"MY MIND MADE ITSELF UP"

Dorothea Lange was born Dorothea Margaretta Nutzhorn on May 26, 1895. The Nutzhorns lived in Hoboken, New Jersey, a one-square-mile town of brownstone row houses built on the banks of the Hudson River, directly opposite New York City. At the time of Dorothea's birth, the population of Hoboken had swelled with the arrival of many immigrants from Europe.

Like many of their neighbors, the Nutzhorn family had their roots in Germany. Dorothea's grandparents made the difficult transatlantic voyage to the United States crowded in the steerage section of a massive ocean liner. Her parents, Henry and Joan, were born in America and were married exactly a year before they had Dorothea.

In 1901, Dorothea's only sibling, her brother Martin, was born. The following year when she was seven, Dorothea was infected with polio. At that time, there was not yet a vaccine to prevent the disease, and she was dangerously sick. When the raging fevers finally left her, her right leg was permanently crippled.

For the rest of her life, Dorothea would walk with a limp. This disability would affect the way she was perceived by others and, in equal measure, how she would view herself. Years later she said, " . . . no one who hasn't lived the life of a semi-cripple knows how much that means. I think it perhaps was the most important thing that happened to me, and formed me, guided me, instructed me, helped me, and humiliated me."[1] To make matters more difficult, Dorothea believed her mother was ashamed of her condition, often scolding her for not walking fully upright. "Walk as well as you can," Joan would whisper to her daughter, worrying, "What would people think?"[2]

As a child, Dorothea felt much closer to her father. One of her fondest memories was of his taking her to a performance of Shakespeare's *A Midsummer Night's Dream*. When they arrived at the playhouse, they found all the seats were already filled. Rather than go home, Henry Nutzhorn lifted Dorothea onto his shoulders and held her there for the entire show. She recalled years after, "that was a magic thing to do for me."[3]

Dorothea Lange was born in this building at 1041 Bloomfield Street, in Hoboken, New Jersey.

But when she was twelve years old, her father abandoned the family. This had to have been a terrible loss for Dorothea. She never chose to speak of his leave-taking at any time during her life, even to those closest to her. Perhaps most tellingly, as a young adult, Dorothea would change her name from Nutzhorn to Lange, dropping her father's name to assume her mother's maiden name instead.

After her husband left her, Joan took the family to live with Dorothea's grandmother. Dorothea described her Grandma Sophie as a "temperamental, difficult, talented woman."[4] She was a dressmaker with a blunt manner of speaking, notorious for telling guests to leave her home as soon as she grew tired of their company.[5]

Sophie was as strong-willed as her daughter Joan was timid. Dorothea felt a tight kinship with her grandmother. Theirs were similarly passionate, perfectionist personalities and what was more, they shared an artistic outlook.

A New York ghetto scene, circa 1902.

Lower East Side

By 1910, more than a half million people lived on the Lower East Side of Manhattan, making it one of the most densely populated areas in the world. Irish and German immigrants began arriving in the mid-nineteenth century, followed a few decades later by Italians and Eastern European Jews. These new urban residents could afford little in the way of housing, and landlords squeezed as many renters as possible into slum dwellings known as tenements. Despite miserable living conditions, the community was a lively one, with its own newspapers, shops, and theaters.

From her grandmother, Dorothea learned the value of a job well done. "It had to be right; you threw it out if it wasn't just right," Dorothea remembered.[6] Sophie observed that her granddaughter had "line in her head," a German phrase meaning that Dorothea was able to appreciate the beauty in everyday objects.[7]

On her birthday one year, an uncle gave Dorothea a bouquet of flowers. Sixty years later, she would recall the enormous pleasure this simple gift had given her: "I sat on the twenty-third street crosstown car, with those lilacs in my lap, jammed in with people, on my birthday, feeling so wonderful . . . the flowers—all my life I don't think I did get over it. I am a passionate lover of flowers. And that's the moment that did it."[8]

Though Joan Nutzhorn was shy, she was capable and she now had a family to support on her own. She found a job as a librarian in a branch of the New York

Public Library on the Lower East Side of Manhattan. She was to be paid twelve dollars a week, a good salary for the time.

Joan began commuting to the city five mornings a week, first crossing the river by ferry and then walking nearly two miles to the library to which she had been assigned. Dorothea made the daily trip with her. While her mother worked, she went to school.

Public School #62 was a big change from the elementary school Dorothea had gone to in Hoboken. For one thing, it was huge. Three thousand students attended the five-story building on Hester Street. For another thing, the students were almost entirely the children of Jewish immigrants.

Dorothea felt like an outsider, "a minority group of one," as she later described it.[9] School had never proved difficult for her before, but her new classmates were more diligent and ambitious than those at her old school. "At P.S. 62, I fell from my perch because I couldn't keep up with them . . . they were hungry after knowledge and achievement."[10]

When classes ended for the day, Dorothea usually went to the library to wait for her mother. Though she was expected to do her homework, more often than not she read books from the library shelves instead. Twice a week her mother had to work late and Dorothea made her way home on her own.

Her return route took her through one of the

Dorothea Lange's mother, Joan, photographed in 1927.

toughest neighborhoods in the city. Unable to run because of her limp, twelve-year-old Dorothea learned to protect herself from danger by making herself appear indifferent to her surroundings. She avoided eye contact and put on what she called her "cloak of invisibility."[11] "I knew how to keep an expression of face that would draw no attention, so no one would look at me," Dorothea explained.[12] When she later became a photographer of people in difficult situations, this skill would prove very useful.

In 1908, when Dorothea was thirteen, the famous modern dancer Isadora Duncan performed at the

Metropolitan Opera House in New York City. For Dorothea, the dancing "was something unparalleled and unforgettable . . . the greatest thing that ever happened."[13]

A few months later, Dorothea started high school. This was to prove a completely forgettable experience. Her new school was called Wadleigh and was located in Harlem, in northernmost Manhattan. It was an all-girls school with nearly four thousand students.

Dorothea would somehow manage to graduate from Wadleigh in 1913, but hers was not a distinguished high school career. Many days she skipped class altogether. She would pretend to go to school, leaving home carrying her books, but spend her hours instead walking through Central Park or finding a free concert or museum exhibit.

Although she had never had a good friend at P.S. 62, at Wadleigh, Dorothea became close with a girl named Florence Ahlstrom, whom she called "Fronsie." Fronsie had long, dark, curly hair and a wide, swishing petticoat that reminded Dorothea of Little Bo Peep. She had never been truant before meeting Dorothea, but she quickly became a constant companion on all of Dorothea's out-of-school activities.

Dorothea was careful not to let her mother or grandmother know she was missing class. In New York City at this time, fully half the school-age children were forced to work instead, almost always for very little pay.

Dorothea was aware of her relative privilege and she admitted to "a heavy conscience."[14]

In addition, many students ended their formal schooling after the eighth grade. During the years Dorothea attended, Wadleigh was one of just three high schools in all of Manhattan. Yet she was aware, too, that what she was learning outside the classroom was every bit as important to her education. She said after, "I realize how enriched I am through having been on the loose in my formative years."[15]

In the months immediately following Dorothea's graduation from high school, her grandmother died and her mother took a new job. Dorothea's relationship with her grandmother had soured somewhat over the years. Sophie drank alcohol excessively and Dorothea and her mother bore the brunt of her abusive language.

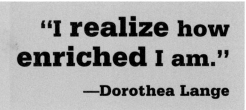

"I realize how enriched I am."

—Dorothea Lange

Now that her daughter had finished high school in the city, Joan Nutzhorn decided she was ready to stop commuting. In 1914, she began working as one of New Jersey's first juvenile court investigators. Her office was near her home in Hudson County.

Joan's responsibilities included making home visitations to ensure that a family was living in a safe environment. Dorothea recalled how difficult and even dangerous her mother's job could be: "I remember my mother going out on streetcars and making night interviews, alone . . . standing on the windy, snowy street corners at night until late because sometimes she would have to wait until the drunken father came home."[16]

To please her mother, Dorothea had returned to school to get a teaching license. Teaching was one of the few professions open to women in the early decades of the twentieth century. Having been deserted by her husband, Joan understood firsthand the importance of a woman being able to make a living for herself. Dorothea and her friend Fronsie enrolled in the New York Training School for Teachers.

Though Dorothea did not question the value of a paycheck, she knew she did not want to become a teacher. Instead she made the rather startling announcement to her family that she had another ambition—she wanted to become a photographer.

Dorothea had never owned a camera or taken a photograph in her life, but for the teenager, the decision was simple. "My mind made itself up. It just came to me that photography would be a good thing for me to do."[17]

3
SAN FRANCISCO SPIRIT

Understandably, Dorothea's mother was very concerned about her daughter's plan. It seemed far-fetched to imagine that Dorothea might be able to support herself as a photographer. She knew absolutely nothing about even the basics of photography, and there were few females in the profession. Joan Nutzhorn insisted Dorothea stay in teacher's college.

At eighteen years old, Dorothea was at a crossroads. She understood that becoming a teacher might appear to be the more sensible route to take, but her heart simply was not in it. At the cusp of adulthood, Dorothea knew she had to follow her instincts.

Almost immediately, she talked her way into a job with a photographer in mid-town Manhattan. Every day when her classes were over, Dorothea went to work at the top-floor studio on Fifth Avenue and Forty-sixth Street. The photographer who owned the business was a man named Arnold Genthe.

Genthe was a renowned portrait photographer. He had first become famous for the photographs he took of the 1906 earthquake that had leveled San Francisco. After the quake, he moved to New York City and opened his portrait studio. He took pictures of the best actors of the day, including Sarah Bernhardt and John Barrymore, and he photographed many important politicians, Presidents Roosevelt, Taft, and Wilson among them.

Dorothea was hired to answer the telephone and print proofs. Proofs are the quick first images made from the photographic negatives. The photographer studies the proofs in order to determine which images, when enlarged, might make the finest photographs. Dust specks often become visible on proofs, and Dorothea learned how to cover them with India ink. She was taught how to mount and frame finished prints as well.

Amold Genthe paid Dorothea fifteen dollars a week, a good salary for the time. Every bit as important as the money, he gave Dorothea her first real lessons in photography. From Genthe, Dorothea learned techniques she would apply in the studio and in the darkroom many times in the years ahead.

A portrait photograph of movie star Greta Garbo taken by Arnold Genthe in 1925.

From Genthe, Dorothea also became aware of a sector of society that was different from that in which she had been raised. His was a "world of privilege," she would later describe, "the most miraculous kind of living, very luxurious, everything of the highest expression."[1]

Dorothea felt the allure of a more sophisticated, artistic culture than she had known in Hoboken. Working at Arnold Genthe's studio confirmed for Dorothea that her gut feelings had been correct. She was determined now to become a photographer in her own right.

The first thing she did was drop out of school. The

final straw was a student teaching arrangement in which the fifth graders she was charged with abruptly left the classroom for the playground without her approval—by way of the fire escape. But even if this humiliating experience had not occurred, Dorothea would have found another reason to leave. She had known from the start that teaching was not for her.

Since she understood that she had a lot to learn about her new chosen profession, Dorothea decided to leave Arnold Genthe's studio to work under another photographer. This second studio, also in New York City just a few blocks north, was a larger and more commercial establishment.

Dorothea was one of several young women whose job it was to make telephone calls to drum up business. Many famous people came to have their portraits done there. Members of the DuPont family, who made their first millions manufacturing gunpowder, were regular customers.

One afternoon, Mrs. DuPont arrived with her many grandchildren in tow to sit for a photograph. The studio gave her a large book to hold on her lap, which was to appear as the family Bible. When the proofs were examined, however, the book could be seen for what it really was: the Manhattan telephone directory. Dorothea was given the responsibility for retouching this picture and disguising the phone book.

To get some hands-on experience with the camera,

Dorothea took another job at a smaller business, unusual in that a woman owned it. The owner was not a photographer herself but someone who hired photographers for jobs. She gave Dorothea her first opportunity to run a photo session on her own. "I was scared to death," Dorothea later recalled. "I was certainly not prepared for it. It was sheer luck and maybe gall."[2] The session ended well and pushed more work Dorothea's way. While she was still an apprentice photographer, she was becoming more confident in her abilities.

A chance encounter at her home with a man selling pictures door-to-door became another important learning experience. This man could not afford a darkroom of his own, but Dorothea recognized that his work had merit, and she helped turn the empty chicken coop in her family's backyard into a darkroom they both could use. From this traveling salesman-photographer, she learned how to develop negatives in a darkroom.

The kind of informal and on-the-job training that Dorothea received was not unusual for the time. While teachers' colleges existed, there were no photography schools. "I invented my own photographic schooling as I went along, stumbling into most of it," she said later.[3]

She did take one course from a prominent photographer named Clarence White who was teaching at Columbia University. Yet even this class was less than traditional in its structure. There was no formal instruction, there were no required assignments, and all work was praised equally. "I don't think he mentioned technique once," Dorothea remembered. "He gave everyone some feeling of encouragement in some peculiar way."[4]

With her earnings from work, Dorothea had been able to buy a new camera and she practiced using it by taking many pictures of her extended family. She viewed herself as any person learning a job, no different than a bricklayer or an electrician. She set high standards for herself, striving to be, as she put it, "very first-class, very top-drawer."[5]

By late 1917, Dorothea believed she was ready to strike out on her own. She was twenty-two years old and eager to leave home for the first time in her life. "I wanted to go away as far as I could go," she remembered.[6] "Not that I was bitterly unhappy at home, or doing what I was doing. But it was a matter

Clarence H. White

At the turn of the last century, Clarence White was part of a small group of prominent photographers who founded the Photo-Secession movement. The Photo-Secessionists believed that the medium of photography was as important a fine art as painting and sculpture. These photographers favored soft lighting and muted scenes, similar to those made by Impressionist artists. In 1914, White opened a school, the first in America to teach photography as an art form. He was known as an open-minded and encouraging teacher who helped bring new standards to photographic design and technique.

Clarence White lectures some students in a studio classroom in 1921.

of really testing yourself out. Could you or couldn't you?"[7]

In January 1918, while World War I devastated Europe, Dorothea and her friend Fronsie Ahlstrom left on a ship that took them from New York to New Orleans. From there, they hopped a train that stopped briefly in Texas and New Mexico before ending its route in California in mid-May.

The young women had a total of one hundred forty dollars between them. On their very first day in San Francisco, Fronsie's wallet was stolen from her purse. They were robbed of all but four dollars.

Barely skipping a beat, Dorothea responded to their predicament by looking in the yellow pages of the telephone book for businesses connected to photography. A department store called Marsh and Company hired her on the spot. Fronsie went to Western Union and got a job sending telegrams. In twenty-four hours the two were employed and their potential crisis averted.

At Marsh's, Dorothea worked behind a high counter at the rear of the store. Her job was to take the orders for film developing. The store sent the film out to a laboratory for printing, and when the pictures came back from the lab, Dorothea was to frame them.

It was not a job she intended to stay at for very long, but it was a job that came at the right time and which ended up being surprisingly meaningful. "That counter was the beginning of my life" in California, she related.[8] "Extraordinary things happened to me over that most unpromising counter."[9]

One of the first customers Dorothea met ended up becoming one of her closest friends for life. His name was Roi Partridge. Partridge was an artist and the husband of a well-known photographer named Imogen Cunningham. Through the couple, Dorothea was soon introduced to other photographers, painters, and writers.

These San Franciscan artists were called Bohemians. The Bohemian lifestyle was free-spirited

> **"Extraordinary things happened to me over that most unpromising counter."**
>
> —Dorothea Lange

and open to new experience. As Dorothea described it, for Bohemians "the rules didn't apply . . . they were the people who lived by their own standards, and did what they wanted to do in the way they wanted to do it."[10]

For a young, independent woman like Dorothea, the Bohemian mold fit perfectly. One of the first things she did was change her last name. She dropped Nutzhorn to become Dorothea Lange instead. Lange was her mother's name before she was married. Dorothea wanted to honor the name of the parent who had raised her, rather than the one who had deserted his family.

She began dressing differently than she had when she lived on the East Coast too. She started wearing long, flowing skirts that were both comfortable and arty-looking. She favored scarves and silver jewelry, and she often topped off her outfit with a black beret.

After only six months working at Marsh's department store, one of Lange's new acquaintances offered her a loan of three thousand dollars so that she might open her own portrait studio. The studio quickly became a successful business as well as a lively gathering place for friends.

Lange installed her darkroom in the basement and

turned the main floor into a welcoming living room. She had a coal-burning fireplace with an overstuffed down sofa facing it. She put out tea and cookies every afternoon at five o'clock, and more often than not, the tea drinkers stayed to listen to records or dance late into the evening.

Many of Lange's customers were wealthy patrons of the artists in her bohemian circle. The studio became known for its celebrity clientele. She worked long hours and was very serious about her work. She said, "I absolutely tried, with every person I photographed, to reveal them as closely as I could."[11]

One night Lange was working in her basement darkroom when she heard distinctive footsteps on the floorboards above her. The clomping sounds came from the cowboy boots of a San Francisco painter named Maynard Dixon. Even apart from his boots, Dixon looked like a cowboy. He was tall and lean, with a sunburned face and a Stetson hat. Dorothea would say later, "He was the kind legends cluster about, without his making any particular effort to nourish them."[12] Dixon was known for his landscape paintings of the West and had traveled widely.

Lange was smitten. Six months later, her studio living room would be transformed with candles and flowers into a makeshift wedding chapel. Dorothea saw her marriage to Dixon as one of equals. To the reporter assigned to cover the story for the San Francisco newspaper, she pronounced solemnly, "My marriage with Mr. Dixon will not interfere with my work, as I shall continue in my profession."[13]

Sometimes even the best-intentioned plans do not work out exactly as expected.

Maynard Dixon

4
REVELATION

When **Dorothea Lange** and Maynard Dixon were married in March 1920, she was twenty-five and he was forty-five. Her friend Imogen Cunningham worried about the big age difference, but Dorothea had her mind made up. "She was strong-willed," Imogen reported, "always fixed in what she thought. Never hesitated about anything."[1]

In the weeks before the wedding, Lange signed up for ballroom dancing lessons. Dancing had always been difficult for her because of her limp. Determined to dance at her wedding and believing the exercise might help her condition, Lange kept at the lessons.

Maynard Dixon had been married once before and had a ten-year-old daughter named Constance, whom everyone called Consie. After Dixon and Lange's four-day honeymoon, Consie came to live with her father. The arrangement proved disastrous.

Lange and Dixon had no time alone to get accustomed to their new life together. He had never been an attentive father. Only twenty-five, Lange had no idea how to raise a school-age child and was not ready to learn. Her photography was her focus.

She tried to please her stepdaughter by taking her to museums and lectures—events she found appealing but the child did not. Much worse, she determined that Consie should learn how to keep house. Lange insisted that the ten-year-old cook, sew, and clean, all to demanding high standards.

Unintentionally, in the first months of her marriage, Lange recreated the Cinderella story. When Consie failed to do her daily chores, Lange became as angry as the evil stepmother in the fairy tale.[2] Before long, Dixon sent his daughter to live with friends.

Aside from the difficult situation with Consie, the couple's first years in San Francisco were good ones. Lange became known as the best studio portraitist in the city.[3] Dixon's paintings sold widely enough that he was able to quit a side job painting billboards for an advertising company.

The couple traveled to the Southwest on a regular basis, staying for weeks at a time. Dixon liked to sketch on location the mountains, canyons, and deserts that

Maynard Dixon's artwork appears here on the cover of *Sunset* magazine.

appeared in his paintings. It was on these trips that Lange took her first photographs outside the studio.

Unlike her husband, Lange was less interested in the landscape of the area than she was in its people. On their trips through the Southwest, she photographed many Navajo and Hopi American Indians.

In the summer of 1923, a very wealthy and eccentric friend of Dixon's named Anita Baldwin invited them to join her on a trip to Arizona. The plans for the trip were to remain a secret even from her guests. Baldwin told the couple only to meet her in Los Angeles and sent them a check to pay for this first leg of the journey.

From there, the group left on a private train with all the shades drawn so no outsiders could see in. Accompanying them was a full staff of bodyguards, cooks, and butlers. The train pulled into Flagstaff, Arizona, at two o'clock in the morning, where yet another group of servants was waiting. Large tents shaped like Chinese pagodas had been set up for sleeping.

At the campsite, dozens of trunks were unloaded from the train. Many of them held the fancy ball gowns and Indian costumes Baldwin planned to wear while camping. Though they were in the middle of the desert, a large number of the trunks were filled with sand. Baldwin had the notion that American

Indians preferred the white sand from California's
ocean beaches.[4]

Each night Baldwin paid the local Indians to
entertain her group with singing and dancing. The
youngest among them were given peacock feathers as
gifts. Baldwin had brought hundreds of these with her
as well.

For the next month, while Dixon painted,
Dorothea Lange photographed. She saw up close how
grim life could be on the reservation. The rich and cel-
ebrated that posed for her in San Francisco were a
world apart from the impoverished Southwest Indians.
For the first time, Lange began entertaining the idea of
using her camera for a different purpose.

Dorothea and Maynard's first son, Daniel Rhodes
Dixon, was born in 1925. Three years later, his brother, John Eaglefeather Dixon, followed him. Having
two small boys to care for, on top of her work at the
studio, was a tall order for Lange. So that she might
have more time for her work, Lange left her sons with
various family friends for long periods at a time. This
was not an easy thing for her to do, but she was
not willing to give up photography for full-time
mothering.

Yet even her photographic work at this time was
not entirely satisfying to her. Lange was losing interest
in making the portraits of her affluent clientele. It paid

the bills, but it was starting to feel less important somehow.

Then, on a family vacation the summer John was one year old, Dorothea Lange had an experience that changed everything for her. She was alone on a cliff, deep in thought, when a severe storm suddenly blew

A photo of an American-Indian girl in a cornfield taken by Dorothea Lange in 1930.

in. She described some time after, "When it broke, there I was, sitting on a big rock—and right in the middle of it, with the thunder bursting and the wind whistling, it came to me that what I had to do was take pictures and concentrate upon people, only people, all kinds of people, people who paid me and people who didn't."[5]

Lange's plans to pursue the different kind of photography she envisioned on the mountainside were put on hold by the massive stock market crash just three months later. The beginning of the economic hard times in America that would be called the Great Depression made it impossible for Lange to switch gears.

In fact, it soon became challenging for her and Dixon merely to make enough money to support their family. Even the wealthy clients who posed for portraits and bought paintings were hit hard by the Depression.

By summertime 1931, Lange decided the family should leave San Francisco for a while. They bought a used Model T car and set off for Taos, New Mexico. Taos was known for its artistic community and appealed as a refuge from the city. "The outside world was full of uncertainty and unrest and trouble," Lange recalled. "We got in the car and we went and we stayed there."[6]

For the Dixon boys, now three and six, New Mexico was a paradise. They had wide-open space in

This portrait photograph of an Hopi Indian man was taken by Dorothea Lange in the late 1920s.

which to run and a pony in the backyard to ride. There, for the first time in their lives, the boys saw snow. "They had been looking forward to the snow," Lange remembered, "and when it came they ran out in it in their pajamas and we had forgotten to tell them it was cold!"[7]

Maynard Dixon borrowed a studio from a friend and went there to paint every day. Lange stayed home in the two-room adobe house with the children, sometimes photographing them but otherwise finding little time for her camera.

During the seven months they spent in Taos, Lange watched the daily comings and goings of a famous photographer named Paul Strand. She noted the sharp difference in their lives. This was a time when women were expected to care for their families before their careers. "That thing that Paul Strand was able to do, I wasn't able to do,"

Taos, New Mexico

In the 1920s, a wealthy heiress from New York named Mabel Dodge Luhan almost single-handedly transformed the quiet Indian pueblo town of Taos, New Mexico, into an international artists' colony. An independent and freethinking woman, Luhan and her third husband, American Indian Tony Luhan, first lured writers Willa Cather and D.H. Lawrence, painter Georgia O'Keefe, and photographers Alfred Stieglitz and Paul Strand to the Southwest. The richness of the Indian and Hispanic cultures, as well as the beautiful desert landscape, encouraged many of the artists to stay and build a vibrant creative community.

Maynard Dixon with his and Dorothea Lange's newborn son, Dan.

she related. "Women rarely can, unless they're not living a woman's life."[8]

When it became too cold for Dixon to paint in the unheated studio (though he tried to hold his brush wearing two pairs of gloves), the family packed up to return north. On the January day before they left, there was a blizzard and they were the first to cut the path down the steep mountain road. It was treacherous, as Lange put it afterward, "seventy-five miles in deep snow with your life in your hands."[9]

Home in San Francisco, the family faced big changes. Lange and Dixon decided against renting a house together, choosing to live in their respective studios instead. Though they were only four and seven years old, their sons were put in a nearby boarding school.

Part of the reasoning behind the decision to live apart was financial. Giving up their house would allow them to save money, but there was more behind the separation—their marriage was in question too.

Sending the boys to live away was an especially hard decision for Lange, but she had come to an understanding of what she must do in order to pursue her career. "Although I didn't like to be separated from the children," she said, "it drove me to work. And I worked

> **"The thing that Paul Strand was able to do, I wasn't . . ."**
>
> —Dorothea Lange

A photo of Lange's young son, Dan, holding out flowers for her on Mother's Day, 1931.

then as I would not have done, I am sure, if I had gone back to my habitual life."[10]

While some people were still able to afford a Lange portrait in 1932, her studio business was slow. By this time, the Depression had stolen the jobs of one of every four Americans. From the window of her second-floor studio, Lange saw huge, milling crowds of these desperate unemployed.

Recalling her moment of insight on the rocks in the thunderstorm, Lange knew instinctively that it was time for her to begin photographing those who could not pay her. She grabbed her camera and went out into the streets.

5

BEYOND
THE STUDIO

It was one thing to view the hordes of poor and hungry from the quiet, safe perch of her studio window. It was quite another to be thrust among them on the noisy streets below.

The people in the streets of San Francisco were frantic with hunger and worry. When the stock market on Wall Street crashed, all they knew and treasured crashed with it. They were out of work, they had lost their homes, and they were unable even to feed their families.

For the first moments on the street, Lange held back from using her camera. "I was not accustomed to jostling about in groups of tormented, depressed and angry men," she related.[1] To overcome her fear, she recalled her school days walking home through the tough neighborhood in New York City. She had learned then how to move through crowds unnoticed. She now put this skill to use once again.

Lange worried that she might hurt someone's feelings taking their picture under such unhappy circumstances. She forced herself to put aside this fear as well: "You quickly forget yourself in your desire to do something that needs to be done," she said simply.[2]

Near Lange's studio a line of men stood waiting to receive a free meal of bread and soup. A wealthy woman who had come to be called the "White Angel" fed them daily. On that first day on the street in 1933, Dorothea Lange took a picture of this bread line.

The photo depicts a grim-faced, huddled group of men in winter coats and hats. At the center of the picture, one man stands with his back to the others. He is unshaven, his hands are clenched together, and he is leaning against a railing. What is striking about this man is his separateness from the group. Among nearly fifteen million unemployed, he stands out as an individual.

From the beginning, Lange understood that just because someone was desperate did not mean they were without pride. "You know that you are not taking anything away from anyone: their privacy, their dignity, their wholeness."[3]

Working on the street was completely different than working in the studio. Instinctive, unposed shots were the opposite of planned, posed portraits. Lange

One of Lange's most iconic photographs, *The White Angel Bread Line*.

had no real idea of what she had captured that very first day. "I can only say I knew I was looking at something," she said later. "You know there are moments such as these when time stands still and all you do is hold your breath and hope it will wait for you."[4]

The White Angel Breadline would become one of the most famous pictures of the Depression era. This photograph marked Lange's shift from one kind of photography to another. From this time on, she would leave the studio more and more to work in the outside world. Two years later, she would close the studio altogether.

Lange and Dixon continued to have difficulties throughout this period. They tried living together again, and they brought the boys home from boarding school for a while, but the marriage remained strained. "I knew that this man loved me and was very, very good to me," she noted. "Still, the depths of his life he didn't share with me. I wasn't really involved with the vitals of the man, not in the vitals."[5]

In the summer of 1934, the streets of San Francisco turned bloody. The dockworkers who loaded and unloaded the ships banded together in a strike against the ship owners. These workers, called long-shoremen, had been forced to toil at extended shifts for exceedingly low pay. When their bosses brought in strikebreakers to work in their stead, violent rioting broke out.

On July 5, 1934, in what became known as "Bloody Thursday," police and strikers battled with tear gas, billy clubs, and bricks. Many men were wounded and two were killed. The governor of California called in the National Guard to occupy the waterfront. Despite the obvious dangers, Dorothea Lange stayed at the docks throughout the chaos to photograph the riots.

That same summer, for the first time, Lange exhibited the new kind of photographs she had been taking. A man named Willard Van Dyke showed the pictures at his gallery. Van Dyke wrote the text for the show, describing the transformation of her work:

A silkscreen version of Anton Refreiger's mural *The Waterfront—1934,* illustrating scenes of dock workers during the 1934 waterfront strike in San Francisco.

*Dorothea Lange has turned to the people of the
American scene with the intention of making an
adequate photographic record of them. These people
are in the midst of great changes—contemporary
problems are reflected on their faces, a tremendous
drama is unfolding before them, and Dorothea
Lange is photographing it through them.*[6]

One of the people who came to see the exhibit was
Paul Taylor, a professor of economics at the University
of California. Taylor was impressed by the work and
asked Lange if she might be interested in taking some
pictures for him.

For over ten years by this time, Taylor had been
studying the problems of migrant workers in
California. He interviewed the agricultural workers in
the fields and wrote up long reports. What he had
never been able to do before, however, was make a useful visual record of his studies.

With Lange's photos accompanying his reports,
Taylor believed the federal government might be more
motivated to assist the migrants. "My *words* would not
be enough, I thought, to show the conditions vividly
and accurately," he related.[7] Lange agreed to assist him.

Paul Taylor had a way of interacting with people
that set them at ease while he interviewed them. He
carried a notebook and jotted down what he was told,
without interrupting or prodding. While some were

This photo was taken by Dorothea Lange during the 1934 waterfront strike in San Francisco. Though standing in the midst of much unrest, this police officer appears composed.

hesitant initially to tell their stories, they soon opened up. "By that time, our relations were all right," Taylor explained. "They had confidence that I was what I said I was. That I was trying to take back to the government, from the people in the field, what they had to say about their own conditions."[8]

Those first days in the field in the fall of 1934, Dorothea Lange observed Taylor, planning to follow his lead. He had years of experience and she was new to the job. In fact, Lange's natural skills at dealing with people allowed her to grasp what was needed immediately.

She had long known how to make herself unobtrusive, how to don what she called her "cloak of invisibility."[9] Lange worked quietly and efficiently, keeping herself in the background. "You know where you're welcome; you know where you're unwelcome," she said later. "But you find your way."[10]

Paul Taylor had wanted a photographer on staff to document his research for a while. He knew that pictures could liven up the dry text and statistics in his reports. But more, he hoped that photographs of the migrants would startle readers and make the workers' plight more real. "There was then a resistance to facing people as human beings," he said. "You free yourself from some responsibilities if you can reduce people to numbers."[11]

Taylor was a man ahead of his time. Using photographs to draw attention to social problems was a new idea. At this time, he was on leave from his university and employed by the government. He was working for an agency called SERA, which stood for State Emergency Relief Administration. When he asked SERA if he might hire a photographer to do the work he envisioned, they said no.

Taylor got around their refusal by putting Lange on the payroll as a typist, even though she had only once taken a three-day typing course and had not typed since.[12] Also, he had only been able to get the agency to agree to fund the job for a month. Lange had to do some good work in a hurry. If she could prove her worth in that short time, Taylor would figure out how to keep her.

Lange, Taylor, and a team of four others spent twelve-hour days interviewing and photographing workers on farms throughout southern California. The work was grueling, "hard, hard living," as Lange put it.[13] The weather was often bad and the sleeping conditions uncomfortable. The farm owners sometimes reacted violently when they tried to speak to the workers.

That first month, Dorothea Lange and Paul Taylor knew they wanted to continue working together. Lange was added to the payroll on a permanent basis. She went back to her family in San Francisco on the weekends, but she spent the workweek with the SERA team.

A date picker's home in Coachella Valley, California, as photographed by Dorothea Lange in 1935.

As the weeks passed, Lange perfected her techniques in the field. Taylor described, "Her method of work was often to saunter up to the people and look around, and then when she saw something that she wanted to photograph, to quietly take her camera, look at it and if she saw that they objected, why, she would close it up and not take a photograph."[14]

She began to converse with the people she photographed as well. That relaxed the workers and made them see that she cared about their welfare. What was more, the exchange helped to make better pictures. "It gave us a chance to meet on common ground," she explained. "Something a photographer like myself must find if he's going to do good work."[15]

Frequently Lange used the migrants' words as captions for her pictures. She was careful always to use their exact words, believing "if you substitute one out of your own vocabulary, it disappears before your eyes."[16]

Just because Paul Taylor had been able to convince SERA to keep Lange on did not mean they were convinced yet of her merit. Taylor included her photographs with every report he made to the agency. With

In the Words of Migrant Workers
(from *An American Exodus*, Lange and Taylor, 1939)

"I put mine in what I thought was the best investment—the good old earth—but we lost on that, too. The finance company caught up with us, the mortgage company caught up with us. Managed to lose $12,000 in three years. My boys have no more future than I have, so far as I can see ahead."

❖ ❖ ❖ ❖ ❖ ❖

"People just can't make it back there, with drought, hailstorms, windstorms, duststorms, insects. People exist here and they can't do that there. You can make it here if you sleep lots and eat little, but it's pretty hard, there are so many people. They chase them out of one camp because they say it isn't sanitary—there's no running water—so people live out here in the brush like a den o' dogs or pigs."

these reports, the team was hoping to build a case for funding to improve the migrants' living conditions.

The typical migrant workers' camp was an inhumane place. There was rarely clean water, and housing was woefully inadequate. What passed for a house was often nothing more than a pile of objects lifted from the city dump. It was the height of the Depression, money was scarce, and the team was uncertain if any would be forthcoming.

It was now fall 1935. Dorothea Lange and Paul Taylor had been working together for a year and were certain of the strength of their professional partnership. Over time, they had realized something else too—they were in love with each other. Both of them had been unhappy in their marriages for a long while.

Lange and Taylor were married at the beginning of December after each received a divorce the month before. Following a quiet ceremony in the morning, Lange went out that same afternoon to photograph. As Taylor would report simply, "Our work went on from then, together."[17]

6

AMERICAN EXODUS

In the months right before they married, Dorothea Lange and Paul Taylor had begun a study of new migrant workers in the state. These workers did not fit the customary mold. Since the mid-nineteenth century, men had been coming to work the fields of California from far-off places like Mexico and the Philippines.

Now not just men but whole families were arriving seeking work. These families were not foreign-born, but had lived instead in Oklahoma, Texas, Missouri, and Arkansas. They were farmers themselves and knew no other life. They came hoping to farm a stranger's land because their own farms had disappeared.

These new migrants were victims of the Great Depression, a seven-year drought, and colossal dust storms that literally blew their farmland away. What was left after the whirling black clouds of dust finally lifted became known as the "dust bowl."

These dust bowl refugees, as the newspapers quickly came to call them, had never been rich. Typically they came from homes without electricity or indoor plumbing, but the Depression had hit them hard and after the dust storms they were left with almost nothing.

More than one million people took to the road and drove west with everything they owned in the back of their trucks.[1] Those not even fortunate enough to own a truck walked or hitchhiked. California seemed to guarantee a better life. The mild climate promised a long growing season and easier living conditions.

In fact, the life they found in California was an extremely difficult one. For families with roots in a homestead for generations, suddenly to be thrown into the role of outsider was painful enough, but more agonizing was the struggle for survival in the crude and overcrowded migrants' camps.

Some families had enough money to rent houses, but poverty forced many others into the camps. There for a few dollars a month a family could rent a tent, a cabin, or a small patch of ground. The camps advertised that they had showers and toilets, but few did and sanitation was a problem everywhere.

These dire living conditions were what Lange and Taylor had begun recording. Their reports

Dorothea Lange at work, shooting on the Texas plains in 1934.

were sent first to the SERA offices in California and then forwarded to a federal agency in Washington, D.C.

The government agency in Washington was called the Farm Security Administration (FSA). Founded in 1935 by President Franklin D. Roosevelt as one of his New Deal programs, the FSA had the stated mission of aiding the many unemployed farmers across the country.

A man named Roy Stryker was responsible for hiring photographers who could help document the plight of the farmers. When Stryker saw Dorothea Lange's work, he asked her immediately to join the FSA staff. Stryker recognized good photography when he saw it. A number of the people he hired—notably Walker Evans, Ben Shahn, and Gordon Parks—along with Lange, would become world-renowned.

Stryker wanted pictures that showed two things: how needy the farmers were and how responsive the government was being in coming to

FDR's New Deal

The New Deal was the name President Franklin Delano Roosevelt gave to the series of programs he created between 1933 and 1937 with the aim of boosting the United States' economy during the Great Depression. These programs were directed to help the failed economy in three ways, known as the "3 R's": with economic relief, recovery, and reform. All over America, millions of unemployed were put to work in engineering, cultural, and agricultural projects sponsored by the federal government.

their relief. For months, Lange and Taylor had been attempting to get the government's attention. Now they had joined forces with Stryker.

Lange began work at the FSA in late February 1936. The first weeks on the job were tough ones for her. She spent fourteen-hour days in the car driving between the farms in the valleys of south-central California. The weather was unusually bleak. She traveled alone, lugging her heavy equipment from the car to the field and back numerous times a day.

After a month's time, Lange was exhausted and decided to take a short break. She packed up her gear and began driving north toward San Francisco. In a hurry to get home, she drove past a sign that read "Pea Pickers' Camp."

Twenty miles farther down the highway, she turned her car around and went back to the camp. Despite her fatigue, the photographer in her had won out. "I was following instinct, not reason," she said later. "I drove into that wet and soggy camp and parked my car like a homing pigeon."[2]

What Lange found at the camp was awful. Whole families crowded together under ripped tarps propped up by tree branches. The migrants had come to pick peas but the harvest had been delayed by frost. Now they were barely surviving on any frozen vegetables they could find in the field to eat.

Lange asked a mother sitting nearby if she might

photograph her. "I do not remember how I explained my presence or my camera to her, but I do remember she asked me no questions," Lange related.[3] "There she sat in that lean-to tent with her children huddled around her, and seemed to know that my pictures might help her, and so she helped me."[4]

The photograph of this tired, worried woman, with an infant in her lap and two older children clutching her on either side, would become the most famous picture ever made by the distinguished Farm Security Administration group. But on this sleeting night, Dorothea Lange did not yet know how many times the photograph, which she would entitle *Migrant Mother*, would be reproduced all over the world. What concerned her then was that people were starving.

She took her photographs to the city editor of the *San Francisco News* the very next morning. She explained the atrocious circumstances of the camp and a story with her pictures appeared in the newspaper the following day. That same week many other newspapers across the country carried the same article.

Migrant Mother brought attention to the predicament of the California dust bowl migrants in an immediate and powerful way. The federal government agreed to send ten tons of food to the pea pickers' camp. To many Americans, *Migrant Mother* became the face they most associated with the crisis of the Depression.

Taken in 1936, Lange's *Migrant Mother* is perhaps her most famous photo. The woman pictured was a thirty-two year old mother of seven and belonged to an impoverished, migrant family of pea pickers.

The farms the migrants worked were not the small, family-owned kind. Rather, they were immense ranches owned by wealthy men who did none of the hard work themselves. Hundreds of workers toiled side-by-side, planting and picking the fruit and vegetables. The weather could be harsh, the labor was grueling, and the wages were minimal.

Since there were always more workers than jobs, migrants were forced to accept the tough conditions and low pay. No matter how tired or hungry or sick they might feel, families had to keep moving, following the work by reading the signs posted along the roads telling them which crops would be harvested next.

Over the next months, Lange and Taylor dispatched many reports to the government, hoping to improve the migrants' lot. Lange believed her pictures would go a long way toward telling the laborers' stories, but she never underestimated the importance of their own words.

"The people who are garrulous and wear their heart on their sleeve and tell you everything, that's one kind of person," she said later, "but the fellow who's hiding behind a tree, and hoping you don't see him, is the fellow that you'd better find out why."[5]

After a four-month stint in California, Lange went to Washington, D.C., to meet for the first time with Roy Stryker. Paul Taylor came with her. At this time he was employed by a different government agency, but his boss and Stryker understood the value of he and Lange working together and finagled the payrolls to allow it.

What to do about their children while they were on the road remained an issue. From his previous

This photo of an African-American family was taken by Lange in early 1939. The family had moved to California from Houston, Texas, two years prior.

marriage, Taylor had three about the same age as Lange's two sons. They rented a big house in Berkeley, and dinners in Chinatown with everyone together around the table were a special treat.[6] When they were away for extended periods, Lange and Taylor were forced to send the children to friends' homes.

In both her marriages, Lange assumed the traditional role of the mother as the primary caregiver. "She was simply superb," Taylor reported, "she made a family out of most diverse relations."[7] But she was "not a liberated woman" entirely either, he admitted.[8]

Roy Stryker suggested Lange and Taylor spend a couple of weeks on the East Coast and then head south. They made a report on unemployed garment workers in New York City and then they crossed the Mason-Dixon line for the rest of the summer.

In what would become a routine for this and the following three summers, 1937–1939, the couple traveled thousands of miles over the back roads of the Deep South, Great Plains, and southwestern United States. They took pictures and recorded stories that they would eventually compile into a book they called *An American Exodus.* This book was one of the first of its kind, devoted to what was newly being described as "photojournalism" or "documentary photography."

There were photographers before this time who had made a case for social change. At the turn of the twentieth century, Jacob Riis exposed the shocking

A Lange photo of Seventh Avenue and West 28th Street in New York in June 1936. The photo shows garment workers leaving their factories for lunch hour.

conditions of tenement life in New York City and Lewis Hine's photos helped to get child labor laws rewritten. But the sheer number of pictures taken by Dorothea Lange and the other Farm Security Administration photographers—over 80,000 in a nine-year period—really brought documentary photography into the mainstream. Before the FSA, few Americans ever saw photographs of social or political upheaval. The FSA's visual record of the Depression was the beginning of modern photojournalism.

For their book, Lange and Taylor chose the word exodus to describe what they referred to as the "unending stream of rural folk" being forced from their land.[9] The authors attributed the exodus to a trio of negative events: the crushing poverty of the Depression, natural disasters like dust storms and drought, and the introduction of tractors to replace human labor.

The more than one hundred photographs and captions in *An American Exodus* are stark. An otherwise

Some photos by Lange, along with accompanying notes from her field reports on the Great Depression.

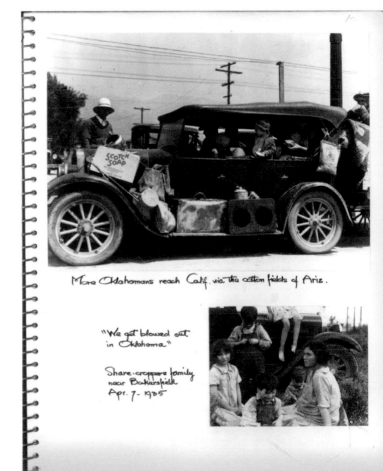

More Oklahomans reach Calif. via the cotton fields of Ariz.

"We got blowed out in Oklahoma"

Share-croppers family near Bakersfield Apr. 7- 1935

unidentified "carrot puller" reports, "They'll sleep in the row to hold a place in the field to earn 60 cents a day."[10] Someone from Macon County, Georgia, jokes ruefully, "A piece of meat in the house would like to scare these children of mine to death."[11]

An American Exodus was published in 1939 to favorable reviews but only modest sales. Yet another book written that same year on the subject of Oklahoma dust bowl migrants became one of the best-sellers of all time. This novel by John Steinbeck was called *The Grapes of Wrath*.

Dorothea Lange's pictures influenced Steinbeck's story.[12] The book's central character is described as looking very much like a migrant in one of Lange's photos. The manager of the migrant camp who treats the family with unexpected respect is based on a real camp manager whom Lange photographed several times. When the famous Hollywood director John Ford prepared his movie version of the book soon after it came out, he used Lange's photographs as inspiration as well.[13]

At the end of 1939, just as it seemed that Lange's authority and effect on others had reached a new high, she received distressing news from Roy Stryker. She was being fired.

7
THE WAR YEARS

The official reason Roy Stryker gave for firing Lange was that he had run out of money to pay her salary, but he was not so short on funds that he had to fire anyone else on his staff, all of whom were men.

The real reasons Stryker let Lange go were that she was a woman and a demanding person. The other FSA photographers were male and traveled together when necessary. Lange traveled alone or with Paul Taylor. As an FSA staffer once noted, "She could not be treated as one of the boys."[1]

More problematic to Stryker was Dorothea Lange's personality. She held exacting high standards for her work that could not always be met with the film and developing processes available at FSA headquarters.

When results were less than perfect, she was never afraid to voice her dissatisfaction. After four years, Stryker had had enough. In a confidential letter to a colleague explaining the firing he wrote, "I selected the person who would give me the least cooperation in the job."[2]

It was now mid-1940. The German "blitzkrieg," or lightning war, had succeeded in conquering most of western and central Europe. President Franklin Roosevelt had begun making preparations for the United States to join the British and Russian forces against the Nazi army.

In San Francisco, Lange found a new job within two months of being let go by the FSA. She was hired as head photographer by another agency of the federal government called the Bureau of Agricultural Economics. This job did not require her to be away as much as before, and she and Taylor decided to buy a house very near to the one they had been renting.

Lange would live in this home at 1163 Euclid Avenue in Berkeley, California, for the rest of her life. The house was built from California redwood and set on a grassy hill amid many trees. She took great pleasure in decorating it and making it comfortable for her family. Lange loved to cook, especially for holidays. Every Thanksgiving and Christmas Eve, large numbers of extended family gathered at long tables to enjoy her feasts.

She had a separate darkroom and studio built behind the house. One entire wall of the studio was paneled with glass, allowing for maximum light. The rest of the space was left open and uncluttered. She told her son, "That's the way I want it. This is where I work, not play."[3]

In March 1941, the prestigious Guggenheim Foundation awarded Lange a yearlong financial scholarship, the first ever given to a woman in photography. She planned to use the grant to study three American rural religious communities. After only four months, however, her work was interrupted.

Her brother Martin had been arrested for insurance fraud and sentenced to a year in prison. A protective sister since their childhood, Lange was devastated. She wrote to the director of the Guggenheim asking for permission to take a short break from her research.

World events then intervened to end the grant work permanently. Two months later, on December 7, 1941, the Japanese Imperial forces bombed Pearl Harbor, the United States naval base in Hawaii. Roosevelt immediately declared war on Japan and its allies, Germany and Italy.

The attack on Pearl Harbor led to frantic speculation that Japan would attack the West Coast of the United States next, with help from Japanese Americans living there. In February 1942, the

This Lange photo was taken on December 8, 1941, the day after the Japanese attack on Pearl Harbor. The sign in window patriotically declares "I am an American."

President authorized the army to "intern" all Americans of Japanese origin. More than 100,000 people were forced from their homes and taken to internment camps in remote parts of the western United States. The camps were little different than prisons.

While the American public generally supported the camps, Dorothea Lange called them "shameful."[4] She believed that the Japanese Americans had broken no laws and were being denied their freedom.

Lange was hired by the government agency in charge of the internment, the War Relocation Authority (WRA), to photograph the evacuation of the

Japanese Americans. That the government would choose to record its actions suggests it had little concern about any wrongdoing. Lange was given no explicit instructions. Perhaps the agency hoped that her photographs would show that the detainees were being well treated.

For eighteen months, she took pictures for the WRA. On the first day she reported, "The people came, with all their luggage and their best clothes and their children dressed as though they were going to an important event."[5] Over time, Lange documented the Japanese Americans in their barracks, in improvised classrooms, and on dusty sandlots playing baseball. While families tried their best to make the day-to-day camp life bearable, the fact that they were living in restricted quarters was never missing from Lange's pictures.

Photographing the wartime internment of Japanese Americans would prove an especially wrenching assignment for Lange. "The deeper I got into it," she recalled, "the bigger it became."[6] Unsurprisingly, in the end the government realized they had made a mistake in hiring someone to chronicle what they were doing and confiscated Lange's pictures. As she described it afterward, "Although the Army wanted a record, it did not want a public record."[7]

The photos were released after the war ended. The photography critic for *The New York Times* admired

Lange photographed these young Japanese Americans upon their arrival at an internment camp in Turlock, California, on May 2, 1942.

Lange's work for the WRA. "She was precisely the right photographer for the job. She functioned in effect as our national eye of conscience in the internment camps. Her constant concerns—the survival of human dignity under impossible conditions . . . were perfectly suited to the subject."[8]

More than any other major American city, San Francisco was changed by the war. With Japan as an enemy, the army and navy bases situated in the West Coast port became important military outposts. The area's shipyards buzzed with new contracts for warships. By war's end, the Bay Area would be the single largest shipbuilding center in the world.

World War II quickly ended the economic problems of the Great Depression. The federal government spent billions of dollars in the San Francisco area alone, shoring up factories, power plants, and highways. The great wave of wartime industrial expansion brought jobs to millions of the unemployed. The migrant workers whom Lange photographed barely surviving five years earlier now took well-paying jobs at the shipyards.

In fact, the war created a serious labor shortage. More than fifteen million people were serving in the military. To fill the shipyard jobs, employers advertised elsewhere for workers. African Americans migrated from the South and large numbers of Mexican workers entered the country and made their way to northern

California. In the absence of so many soldiers, thousands of women went to work for the shipbuilders as well.

Dorothea Lange lived very near the largest of the shipyards in a city named Richmond. Her brother Martin, now out of jail, and her son Dan, both had jobs there. In 1944, *Fortune* magazine hired her to photograph the Richmond yards. The magazine hired another famous photographer to work with her. His name was Ansel Adams.

"She was **precisely the right photographer for the job.**"—A.D. Coleman, *New York Times* photography critic.

Adams was best known for his sweeping landscape photographs, many of which were taken in California's Yosemite Valley. He was a dedicated environmentalist and a leader of the Sierra Club, an organization founded to protect the wilderness.

He and Lange had known each other for years but had never before shared an assignment. Adams had also taken pictures of the interned Japanese Americans for the WRA, but unlike Lange, he believed their relocation had been justifiable in light of the war.

The photographers parted ways in their working habits too. Ansel Adams fixed his cumbersome equipment on a raised platform and enjoyed the limelight of people watching him at work. Lange liked to fade into a crowd with a small portable camera in hand. An assistant at the shipyard photo session reported they "were an impossible team, they were so unlike each other."9

In the photographs he took at Richmond, Adams focused on the impressive ships and booming industry at the yard. With her very different perspective, Lange's

Shipyard workers photographed by Lange in 1943.

Victory Magazine

Dorothea Lange and Ansel Adams also collaborated on a number of photography projects for a magazine called *Victory*. Published by the federal Office of War Information for the purpose of spreading "the American spirit to war-torn Europe," copies of *Victory* were air-dropped by planes into European towns in the days immediately preceding the arrival of Allied troops. The Office of War Information hoped *Victory* might pave the way to a warmer welcome for the soldiers from local villagers.

pictures comment on the separateness of the people's lives. Many of her photos show workers between shifts, walking to and from the factory with no evident interaction.

In April 1945, San Francisco was host to the first meetings of the newly formed United Nations. Lange was asked to photograph the important conference. For some time, she had been suffering from severe unexplained stomach pain. Her doctor warned her not to work too hard. "Take it easy?" she scoffed. "How can a photographer take it easy?"[10]

World War II ended in August 1945. That same month, Lange had her gallbladder removed but found no relief from the acute stomach pain. Four weeks later, she was rushed back to the hospital with internal bleeding. "It was a terrible time," Paul Taylor said later, "we thought we had lost her."[11]

The doctors determined that Lange had an ulcer, an inflammation of her stomach, and they performed surgery to save her life. The recovery from this surgery was difficult. Lange tried to show a cheerful face to her family but confided to her diary, "This is the simple fact. I endure pain a part of every day. This leaves exhaustion. It hurts me. Sometimes, if I am alone, I cry out. Sometimes I am stronger and can endure it."[12]

It would be a very long time before she felt strong enough to work again.

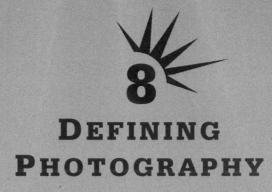

8

DEFINING PHOTOGRAPHY

Т
he next years were tough ones for Lange. She simply did not have the strength to go out into the field to take pictures. She was forced to spend many of her days entirely in bed. But ever the photographer, she turned her camera on what she still could observe around her.

Her focus switched from the outside world and its larger social problems to the nearer, personal world of her family and friends. She described, "Instead of photographing men in relation to events, as I have, today I'm trying to photograph men in relation to men, to prove the exchanges and communications between people, to discover what they mean to each other and to themselves."[1]

Most of these photographs would go no further than

Lange's file drawer. At this time, there was not a lot of interest among photographic publications or the general public for pictures of domestic scenes. Photographs of the Depression or dust bowl refugees were one thing, pictures of Lange's firstborn grandchild or the enormous maple tree in her backyard were quite another.

In 1951, Lange escaped the confines of home to speak at a national conference on photography. The most prominent photographers in the country assembled in Aspen, Colorado, to exchange ideas on the role and meaning of their work.

Dorothea Lange asked the group if they might supply a better term than "documentary" to describe the work she and others had been doing. Lange argued that the documentary photographer did not merely record, or document, but also informed and characterized events.[2]

"For me documentary photography is less a matter of *subject* and more a matter of *approach*," Lange explained. "The important thing is not *what's* photographed but *how* . . . My own approach is based on three considerations. First—hands off! Whatever I photograph, I do not molest or tamper with or arrange. Second—a sense of place. Whatever I photograph, I try to picture as part of its surroundings, as having roots. Third—a sense of time. Whatever I photograph, I try church members to show as having its position in the past or in the present."[3]

The panel of photographers was unable to come up with another expression, but the discussion itself proved meaningful. The director of the Museum of Modern Art's photography department reported, "Nothing as intense or inspiring has ever happened to a group of persons in and around photography."[4]

Before the ten-day conference came to a close, the photographers agreed to publish, for the first time, a professional journal they decided to call *Aperture*. It exists to this day as one of the most important fine art photography magazines. As one of the original co-founders, Lange played a vital role in its release.

The next fall, Lange's mother died at home in New Jersey. She was seventy-nine years old. Coincidentally, Lange was in New York City at the time to discuss the inclusion of thirty-six of her photographs in an exhibit at the Museum of Modern Art. This museum show was one of the largest of its kind, devoted solely to the work of prominent photographers.

By 1954, Lange finally felt healthy enough to spend an extended period of time in the field. She agreed to do some work for *Life* magazine. *Life* was an extremely popular weekly with millions of readers. Dedicated to covering current events and feature stories primarily through photographs, *Life* had been published for almost twenty years by this time, but

Lange had never before been asked to contribute to the magazine.

For the first assignment, she teamed up again with Ansel Adams. They drove to Utah to take pictures of the Mormons, the followers of The Church of Jesus Christ of Latter-day Saints. The pair easily divided their work by what they did best: Adams photographed the mountainous landscape and isolated towns, while Lange concentrated on the people.

At one of the small churches, some elderly parishioners blocked Lange at the door, uncomfortable with the idea of any

Two Mormon businessmen photographed by Dorothea Lange in 1953.

church members being photographed. Thinking quickly, she asked Paul Taylor, who had accompanied her on the trip, to go into the church and sit down in a pew. Thrilled by the thought of a potential new member to their church, the group followed Taylor in and left Lange to take her pictures.

The Mormon story appeared in *Life* the first week of September. Lange was already in County Clare, Ireland, working on a second assignment for the magazine. Her son Dan went with her this time, acting as her assistant and taking notes. Very much enjoying her month there, she focused on Irish farm families and their deep-rooted connectedness to the land.

The work she did for *Life* was very different for Dorothea Lange than the work she had done for the government. Her husband explained the key distinction: "When she was doing an article for *Life* she was focusing on a narrower subject; when she was out in the field photographing for the government, it was catch as catch can."[5]

By this time, most professional photographers were using the newer 35-millimeter camera. While Lange owned one and used it at home, on the job she remained loyal to the older format cameras with which she felt more comfortable. In a similar vein, she used only black-and-white film and avoided a flash at any cost. To her mind, the natural light of a photograph was one of its essential characteristics.[6]

Surprisingly, Lange was not known for her technical expertise. While Ansel Adams took painstaking measurements with his light meter, Lange would look up at the sky and guess.[7] A longtime assistant of hers joked about her technical incompetence but noted it never mattered in the end: "She could use an old film pack or pull the wrong lever. Yet when it was over, she had the picture she wanted. She had to go to great pains to make a good print. It took her an endless amount of time. But look at the results."[8]

In January 1955, a large photography show opened at the Museum of Modern Art in New York City. Called "The Family of Man," the exhibit included over five hundred pictures of people from all over the world. In the aftermath of World War II, the show's curator, Edward Steichen,

Lange's Camera: Technical Specifications

"For equipment she uses two cameras. On any given trip she takes one or the other with her, never both. One of these is a 3 1/4 x 4 1/4 Graflex equipped with a 7 1/2 inch focal length anastigmat lens and magazine film holders, the other a Rolleiflex which she considers to have a general advantage in that it is less obtrusive and can be operated at closer quarters. The latter, of course, by virtue of the smallness of the film does not permit as great a degree of enlargement. She uses a Weston exposure meter to test the general light conditions once or twice during the expedition."
—Willard Van Dyke, *Camera Craft*, October 1934

meant to demonstrate the many shared experiences that connected different cultures.

Lange worked closely with Steichen for the two years preceding the exhibit's opening. She helped to solicit photos and to choose from among the tens of thousands offered. Hers was one of the few opinions the curator regularly sought.[9] Lange recalled the hectic pace of their preparation, up to the last minute: "He worked up to a terrific climax where everybody doesn't sleep for three or four days and they work day and night and they live on black coffee and he gets it done . . . on the afternoon of the day when the show was opening they were still making prints."[10]

Dorothea Lange had nine pictures in the show, including *White Angel Breadline* and *Migrant Mother*. After four months in New York, "The Family of Man" toured the world for eight years, on view in thirty-seven countries on six continents. It was by far the most popular photography show ever assembled. The book produced from the show, still in print today, has sold more than five million copies, more than any other photographic title.

As soon as "The Family of Man" opened in New York, Lange returned to California and began working on a photographic essay for *Life*. Entitled "Public Defender," the piece was to follow the daily activities of an attorney named Martin Pulich, whose job it was to defend in court prisoners who could not otherwise afford a lawyer.

Taking pictures of people who were in jail awaiting trial was similar in many ways to photographing the dust bowl migrants or the interned Japanese. All had been deprived of their former lives. Lange went to

This Lange photo, snapped in 1957, is titled *Berryessa— Water Coming In.*

courtrooms and jail cells for a year, assembling her story.

In the end however, *Life* decided not to use the article. The editors thought Lange's pictures were good but did not tell the kind of specific story the magazine preferred. Instead of focusing on Pulich, or one or two prisoners, Lange chose to show generally how difficult a disadvantaged life could be.

She sold some of the photographs to a legal aid society and some newspapers bought others, with a new story centered on Martin Pulich, but the huge audience *Life* would have guaranteed never saw the full extent of her efforts on this essay.

Without stopping for a break between assignments, Lange agreed next to a forty-page piece for *Aperture* magazine. On this she collaborated with a former assistant of Ansel Adams, a man named Pirkle Jones.

The two photographers chose as their subject the ecology of the Berryessa Valley, some fifty miles north of San Francisco. A place of great natural beauty, the quiet valley was dotted with farms, ranches, and orchards. Only one small town existed in the area, but developers had big plans.

Builders intended to construct new homes along with a dam, which would act as a reservoir supplying water to the growing population. The dam would submerge everything in its wake. In the months before the construction began, Lange and Jones documented the signs of impending change: families moving, farmers auctioning off their heavy equipment, and ranchers selling off their cattle.

The photographers did not stop when the tractors moved in. Their pictures showed the absolute destruction of the land once the dam was completed. As she had done with the captions for the pictures of the dust bowl migrants, Lange was careful to use the exact words of those she photographed. One man lamented, "Everyone said they'd never flood it. Even when they talked about it, we never believed they'd flood it."[11]

Lange and Jones were ahead of their time with a story on environmental misuse. Today concern for the land is widespread, but in the late 1950s, what the article bemoaned "the price of progress" was a relatively new issue.[12]

Lange was sick the entire time she was in the Berryessa Valley. Her stomach problems continued to plague her, making eating even the blandest foods a chore. The valley's temperature fluctuated wildly too, with heat extremes well above one hundred degrees. Between her ill health and the weather, it was an especially difficult trip.

With the *Aperture* project finished, Lange thought she would be better off staying home for a while. When she was offered a part-time teaching position at the California School of Fine Arts, she accepted. Though she had not wanted to teach as a young woman, now at sixty-two, she viewed the job differently.

With a lifetime of experience and a passion for her subject, Lange took easily to her new role. She rarely lectured, instead setting an intentionally loose tone in the classroom. The first day she posed the single question that she wanted answered differently each week through pictures; this question was, "Where do you live?"

From a photographic seminar held in Aspen, Colorado, in 1951. Left to right, back row: Herbert Bayer, Eliot Porter, Joella Bayer, Mrs. Paul Vanderbilt, Connie Steele, John Morris, Ferenc Berko, Laura Gilpin, Fritz Kaesér, Paul Vanderbilt; center: Mrs. Eliot Porter and Minor White; front row: Ansel Adams, Dorothea Lange, Walter Paepcke, Berenice Abbott, Frederick Sommer; Nancy and Beaumont Newhall; on floor: Will Connell and Wayne Miller.

Through this inquiry, Lange wanted her students to reconsider the everyday objects in their homes and contemplate their significance. A messy desktop, for example, or a vase of flowers past their prime, had meaning beyond the obvious. "Bring the viewer to your side," she told them, "include him in your thought. He is not a bystander. You have the power to increase his perceptions and conceptions."[13]

In 1957, this was an unorthodox way to teach. Most photography classes at this time taught the mechanical aspects of using a camera and little else, but for Lange the technical side of photography was never the most important. "The good photograph," she reminded her students over and over, "is not the object. The consequences of that photograph are the object."[14]

9
RETROSPECTIVE

Dorothea Lange and Paul Taylor had a rustic two-room cabin they liked to go to on the weekends. Built on the sand dunes overlooking the Pacific, the cabin had a name—Steep Ravine—but it had neither a telephone nor any electrical power.

Steep Ravine was a favorite spot of Lange and Taylor's grandchildren. The children spent their days on the beach collecting driftwood and sea glass. At night they curled up in their sleeping bags and listened to stories. They were very much accustomed to their grandmother taking photographs of them. Most of these were casual pictures, intended as family mementos, but others were planned as part of a family-themed project Lange worked on over the last ten years of her life.

She called this work-in-progress "To a Cabin." The photographs that became part of this grouping centered on the daily activities of her extended clan. While family had always been important to Lange, as she grew older the rituals of family life held a particular significance for her.

In mid-1958, Lange made plans to leave the country for only the second time in her life. Paul Taylor had been offered a six-month job in Asia. Lange had mixed emotions about going. For one thing, she knew she would sorely miss her family. For another, she was worried about her health.

Regarding her chronic condition, her doctor bluntly allayed her fears. "What does it matter," he asked her, "if you die here or there?"[1] To the practical-minded Lange, the doctor's logic made good sense.

The couple flew from San Francisco to Seoul, Korea, where Taylor planned to work for the first two months. Korea was an exotic place for Lange that she tried to photograph without much luck. "I cannot go out into the streets unaccompanied," she complained. "I am surrounded, my clothes examined, my hair stroked. I am a novelty, and the camera just tops it off."[2]

Their next stops in Bali, Indonesia, and Calcutta, India, were somewhat different experiences. Here Lange was free to take pictures but still felt hindered. Having worked independently for so long, she was

A street scene photo taken by Lange during her trip to Asia in 1958.

frustrated by the limits her husband's schedule imposed. While she felt fortunate to be with him abroad, the photographer in her was vexed by the images she perceived but was not able to stop and carefully record.

"There is dust on the cameras," she related, "because I do not want to make snapshots as we tear about, from one province to the other."[3] To Lange, a snapshot was a hurried, random picture, not the deliberate photograph of a professional.

After five months in Asia, Lange and Taylor spent eight more weeks driving around Europe in a Volkswagen bus. For much of this time, Lange was ill. Frequent fevers and stomach pains kept her in bed for days on end. Yet her report to the family upon their return home was glowing. She announced to them all, "I am a woman who has been around the world."[4]

However, when Paul Taylor went to Cuba over the summer to do some work for the new government there under Fidel Castro, Lange stayed put. She continued photographing the family for her study. A year later, when her husband was again asked to head a project overseas, she felt healthy enough to accompany him. This time the two headed south to Ecuador and Venezuela.

Lange was intrigued by the cultural diversity in South America. She photographed many landscapes of churches, markets, and farms. Still, as had always been the case for her, it was the people she encountered that she found most compelling. These subjects were not the rich and famous but ordinary citizens. "The chances of getting a photograph when you're going to the drugstore for a tube of toothpaste are better than when you're hanging out on the street corner waiting for the next great photograph," she said.[5]

When Lange returned home to California, she discovered to her enormous disappointment that her camera had not been working correctly the whole time she was away. Many of the pictures she took in South America could not be developed as she had hoped.

Fortunately, a magazine asked to publish the pictures she had taken in Asia. Lange went to work immediately writing captions and editing images from the earlier trip. Entitled "Remembrance of Asia," the photo essay appeared in *Photography Annual.* An exhibition of the pictures was shown also at a Boston gallery in the spring of 1961.

During the same period, 1960–1961, Lange began recording the story of her life for the University of California at Berkeley. The university had established an oral history department devoted to interviewing important Californians.

Lange was interviewed eleven times over the year. While it was not always easy for her to discuss certain aspects of her life, she admitted she was interested in doing the history and compared herself to "people who maintain they don't like to have their picture taken [but] usually really do like it."[6]

In May 1962, after forty years at the University of California, Paul Taylor retired. He did not plan, however, to give up teaching altogether. The University of Alexandria in Egypt had offered him a one-year position as a visiting professor.

Dorothea Lange did not want to go to Egypt. She was sick and knew she did not have many years left to spend with her family, but she did not want to be away from her husband either. To an interviewer she admitted, "I'd like to take one year . . . just one, when I would not have to take into account anything but my own inner demands . . . but I can't."[7]

Egypt proved exhilarating and exasperating at the same time. From their eighth floor penthouse apartment, the couple could look down on the city and the blue Mediterranean Sea. Taylor's job provided them with a cook and a driver. Yet in the narrow streets, a tougher existence awaited. As a foreigner, Lange was made to feel unwelcome. She was harassed constantly when she tried to take pictures. One day, children even threw stones at her.

As much as the pestering bothered her, it was not completely unexpected. Lange had always been aware of the fact that photography was intimidating to many people. For a person unsure of a photographer's motives, having a picture taken could be uncomfortable. Lange claimed she fully understood "a person *really* wanting to know what the dickens you were doing with a camera when you stand in a strange country surrounded by people you don't know."[8]

Despite the difficulties in Egypt, by the time they left the country Lange had somehow managed to take over two thousand pictures. Unfortunately, though she did not know it yet, she also had contracted malaria. The subsequent weeks of travel were terrifying ones.

In Iran, the next country on their itinerary, Lange ran a fever of 103 and began hallucinating. The antibiotics they gave her in the hospital brought the fever under control and the worst was presumed over. A few days later in Switzerland, however, it

The Museum of Modern Art Retrospective

Prior to Lange, the New York Museum of Modern Art had assembled only five "one-man" photography shows and all of the photographers had, in fact, been men. Lange was in good company: the photographers who preceded her with museum retrospectives were Walker Evans, Paul Strand, Edward Weston, Henri Cartier-Bresson, and Edward Steichen. With her retrospective, however, Lange hoped to leave her own mark. "In this show," Lange explained in the documentary *Under The Trees*, "I would like to be speaking to others in the sound of my own voice, poor though it may be. Not other people's voices."

became clear that the relief had been premature.

Paul Taylor recalled the frightening drive he made rushing his wife back to the hospital. "I sweated blood on the way as the temperature continued to go up, up, up, with Dorothea in the back seat and me driving through Switzerland on those mountainous roads."[9] The doctors diagnosed Lange's condition and began treatment. Hers was only the second case of malaria ever identified at that time in Switzerland.

After three weeks of malaria medicine, Lange finally was well enough to return to the United States. The pace of travel plus the malaria, on top of the chronic illness she had been enduring for years, had tired her out. She was very glad to be home, and she made plans for an exhibit she had been holding off doing for some time.

The Museum of Modern Art in New York

Lange and her family during summer vacation at Steep Ravine in September 1957.

long had wanted to do a retrospective of Lange's career. A retrospective is a museum show that includes examples from all periods of an artist's life. Before this time, Lange had believed that she was not ready for such a show, that there was still more work she planned to do.

At this point in her life, Lange knew her most productive days were over. She agreed to begin pouring over the tens of thousands of negatives she had in her files. Choosing which photographs to include in the exhibit would not be an easy task for her. "A photographer's files are in a sense his autobiography," she related. "More resides there than he is aware of."[10]

Then soon after Lange started work, she received word from her doctor that she had inoperable cancer. While the doctor could not predict exactly how much longer she might live, he made it clear that time was short.

The photography curator at the Museum of Modern Art, John Szarkowski, flew out from New York City to help Lange review her files. They affixed a long bulletin board to one of the walls of her living room. In her weakened state, Lange rested on the couch while Szarkowski tacked up groupings of photographs for her approval. Lange was the

Dorothea Lange in the studio in May 1964.

toughest critic of her own work. "Not good enough, Dorothea," she would say, shaking her head. "'A' for effort, that's all."[11]

During much of their collaboration, Lange and Szarkowski were filmed for a documentary entitled *Under the Trees*, commissioned by the San Francisco public television station. The camera crew was allowed to be present in the living room while the daily photo editing process proceeded, but they were not otherwise permitted to interfere.

A number of technical assistants helped make prints and enlargements. One of them later spoke of his admiration for Lange's work ethic despite the great pain her illness was obviously causing her. The assistant said he "could feel the sheer driving force and determination of this remarkable woman."[12]

In any exhibition, but particularly one with the magnitude of a retrospective, the give-and-take between artist and curator is very important. Though neither ever hesitated to voice an opinion, Lange and Szarkowski worked well together. Lange tended to opt for pictures that she believed best told the story of their time, while Szarkowski stuck with the single images he believed made the strongest impression.[13] When they finished, in appreciation to the curator for his help, Lange presented him with a treasured gong she had brought home from Asia.

The two hundred photographs that made the final

cut for the exhibition spanned four decades of Lange's career, from the 1930s to the 1960s. The pictures were grouped by subject or chronology, with captions kept to a bare minimum. Lange had insisted that the words under the pictures be few so as not to overly influence the viewer.[14]

On October 11, 1965, just a few days after the first exhibition prints were made, Dorothea Lange died at seventy years old. She had worked very hard until the end and the effort brought additional meaning to her last days. Paul Taylor reported her last words, "This is the *right* time. Isn't it a miracle that it comes at the right time!"[15]

10

ENDURING
RECORD

In the last two years of her life, Dorothea Lange tried to propel into motion two major undertakings. While neither ended up receiving the necessary funding, both prove Lange's passionate dedication to her field and her high hopes for the future of photography.

She called her plans simply Project I and Project II. The aim of Project I was to hire a group of young photographers to chronicle everyday life in America's cities over a five-year period. As the Farm Security Administration photographers had done for the 1930s, Lange envisioned a new team doing for the 1960s.

"No young photographers have had the training and the education and the experience that we had," she explained. "That's deplorable. The younger people should have the same chance we had."[1] She planned for the photographs to become part of the Library of Congress' permanent collection and an important research resource for historians, teachers, and artists.[2]

The idea behind Project II was the creation of a photography center to train students, museum curators, librarians, and others, both professional and amateur, in the field of photography. Lange was less interested in the center being a school in which techniques were stressed as a place where people, as she put it, "learn *to see*."[3]

For Lange, learning to see meant examining the world with the heart as much as the mind. The technical aspects of photography never interested her in the way that its emotional aspects did. She understood that a photograph did not have to be technically perfect for it to have a strong and lasting impact on the viewer.

What was more, seeing people and events as they truly were—and not necessarily how the photographer might want them to be—was a guiding principle for her. On the wall of her studio she posted a quotation attributed to Sir Francis Bacon, the sixteenth century English philosopher. It read:

> *The contemplation of things as they are, without substitution or imposture, without error or confusion, is in itself a nobler thing than a whole harvest of invention.*[4]

Some of Dorothea Lange's best work on display at the Franklin D. Roosevelt Presidential Library and Museum in Hyde Park, New York, on November 2, 2004.

Throughout her career, Lange's first task as a photographer was to record rather than to create. Her pictures were documents, not decorations. From her earliest days in the studio, she described herself simply as a person plying a trade. "I've denied the role of artist. It embarrassed me, and I didn't know what they were talking about," she claimed.[5]

It was only in the final years of her life that she was willing to concede that there was something more to her photography, "a 'plus-something' that happens when your work is done, if it's done well enough, and intensely enough."[6] As her husband, economist Paul

Taylor, corroborated, "in her last years, when she reviewed her life, she evaluated herself properly. Not flaunting it, not in any sense; simply evaluating herself truly, and she was right."[7]

Dorothea Lange's pictures from the Depression era are among the most enduring and important of all photographic records. Her *Migrant Mother* is one of the most reproduced images in the world. Yet the very fame of this picture bears out Lange's contention that she was first a documenter of events and only secondarily an artist.

In his introductory essay for her retrospective exhibit at the Museum of Modern Art, curator George P. Elliott explained it this way:

> Migrant Mother *is famous because key people, editors and so on, themselves finding it inexhaustibly rich, have urged the rest of the world to look at it. This picture, like a few others of a few other photographers, leads a life of its own. That is, it is widely accepted as a work of art with its own message rather than its maker's; far more people know the picture than know who made it.*[8]

Of course, Lange's photographs for the Farm Security Administration did far more than create famous images. Her pictures persuaded the federal government to provide the money needed for relief programs that helped tens of thousands of desperately poor Americans.

Though they were often homeless and destitute, Lange never deprived her subjects of their personal dignity. In her photographs of the San Francisco unemployed workers, the dust bowl refugees, and again later with the interned Japanese Americans, she revealed the courage and pride of distinct individuals.

Lange was an impulsive, pioneering woman. She decided to become a photographer—a profession then dominated by men—before she had ever taken a

A shot of the Tin Can Diner in Venango, Nebraska, taken by the 2006 Lange-Taylor prizewinner, Peter Brown.

single picture. At twenty-two, she moved cross-country where she knew no one, joining a group of Bohemian artists. Twelve years later, when the stock market crashed and money for her portrait studio dried up, she took her camera into the streets.

Despite the expectation of her time that mothers were the parent responsible for staying home with the family, Lange managed a full-time career. This was never an easy situation and required painful compromise for her and her children. In the field, she and husband Paul Taylor were a team of equals. Outside of work, he acknowledged, "She was harnessed to the house."[9]

Still, Lange attended to her family with the same intense energy and discipline she gave to her work. At her funeral, her son Daniel Dixon expressed his deep appreciation for her devotion. "The highly colored details of family life—nothing was more important to her . . . In this way, too, she had genius."[10]

Over three decades, Lange's commitment to photography as a way to help people and bring about social change was unwavering. Together with her husband, Paul Taylor, she worked to combat poverty and improve the lives of those she called "the voiceless."[11]

FSA photographers were charged with making "an historical picture of America in photographs."[12] Lange always took this part of her job very seriously. For her, the creation of an archive for future generations was as important as instigating change in the present. "Documentary photography records the social scene of our time," she stated. "It mirrors the present and documents for the future."[13]

Lange's method of working was honest and compassionate. She traveled to find those in need, she listened carefully to their stories, and she made certain she had her subjects' cooperation before taking a picture. She was open-minded and flexible: "To know ahead of time what you're looking for means you're then only photographing your own preconceptions, which is very limiting and often false," she once explained.[14]

In a time before television, Lange's photographs were among the most powerful visual images of social conflict that most Americans had ever seen. She understood the influence of photography as a force for social and political change and she wielded this power to great effect.

Dorothea Lange's photographs helped shape history and photography shaped her life. Hers was a simple description of a complex and fulfilling life: "You put your camera around your neck in the morning along with putting on your shoes, and there it is, an appendage of the body that shares your life with you."[15]

CHRONOLOGY

1895 Dorothea Margaretta Nutzhorn is born on May 26 in Hoboken, New Jersey.

1902 Contracts polio that leaves her with a permanent limp.

1907 Father abandons family. Dorothea moves with her brother and mother into her grandmother's house.

1912 Enrolls briefly in Teachers' College then determines to pursue a career in photography despite the fact that she has never used a camera.

1913 Takes job with renowned portrait photographer Arnold Genthe.

1918 Moves to San Francisco, becomes part of Bohemian artists' group. Changes last name from Nutzhorn to Lange.

1919 Opens own portrait studio.

1920 Marries Maynard Dixon. Begins regular travel to southwestern United States.

1925 Son Daniel Rhodes Dixon born.

1928 Son John Eaglefeather Dixon born.

1929 Lange envisions for herself a new form of photography outside the portrait studio. Stock market crash ushers in Great Depression.

1931 Family moves to Taos, New Mexico, for seven months.

1932 Lange takes her first photographs on the streets of San Francisco.

1933 *White Angel Breadline* marks success of new photographic focus.

1934 Successful gallery showing. Begins working in migrant camps with economist Paul Taylor.

1935 Lange and Taylor divorce spouses and marry.

1936 Begins work documenting farmers for the Farm Security Administration (FSA). Takes famous photograph *Migrant Mother*.

1937–1939 Summer travel throughout rural U.S. creating new documentary photography. *An American Exodus* published. Lange fired from FSA.

1940 Hired by Bureau of Agricultural Economics. Moved with family to new home in Berkeley, California.

1941 Awarded Guggenheim scholarship. Pearl Harbor attacked.

1942 Hired by War Relocation Authority to photograph internment camps holding Japanese Americans.

1944 *Fortune* magazine assignment with Ansel Adams.

1945–1950 Ill health makes work difficult.

1951 Participates in national conference on photography.

1954 *Life* magazine assignments.

1955 Collaborates in "The Family of Man" exhibition.

1957 Teaches photography classes at California School of Fine Arts.

1958 International travel with Paul Taylor.

1960–1961 Oral history for the University of California at Berkeley.

1964 Prepares retrospective for Museum of Modern Art.

1965 Dies on October 11 at age seventy.

CHAPTER NOTES

Chapter 1. Heartbreak in the Heartland

1. Richard K. Doud, interview with Dorothea Lange, Archives of American Art, Smithsonian Institution, May 22, 1964, p. 9.

Chapter 2. "My Mind Made Itself Up"

1. Suzanne Reiss, "Dorothea Lange: The Making of a Documentary Photographer," an interview with Dorothea Lange (1960–1961), Regional Oral History Office, University of California, Berkeley, 1968, p. 17.

2. Ibid., p. 6.

3. Milton Meltzer, *Dorothea Lange: A Photographer's Life* (Syracuse, N.Y.: Syracuse University Press, 2000), p. 8.

4. Ibid., p. 5.

5. Elizabeth Partridge, *Restless Spirit: The Life and Work of Dorothea Lange* (New York: Viking, 1998), p. 10.

6. Meltzer, p. 5.

7. Partridge, p. 11.

8. Reiss interview, pp. 21–22.

9. Ibid., p. 13.

10. Ibid.

11. Partridge, p. 13.

12. Reiss interview, p. 16.

13. Ibid.

14. Reiss interview, p. 26.

15. Ibid., p. 27.

16. Meltzer, p. 19.

17. Ibid., p. 23.

Chapter 3. San Francisco Spirit

1. Suzanne Reiss, "Dorothea Lange: The Making of a Documentary Photographer," an interview with Dorothea Lange (1960–1961), Regional Oral History Office, University of California, Berkeley, 1968, p. 28.

2. Ibid., p. 34.

3. Milton Meltzer, *Dorothea Lange: A Photographer's Life* (Syracuse, N.Y.: Syracuse University Press, 2000), p. 28.

4. Reiss interview, p. 40.

5. Ibid., p. 76.

6. Elizabeth Partridge, *Restless Spirit: The Life and Work of Dorothea Lange* (New York: Viking, 1998), p. 20.

7. Ibid.

8. Reiss interview, p. 86.

9. Ibid.

10. Ibid., pp. 105–106.

11. Meltzer, p. 49.

12. Ibid., p. 52.

13. Ibid.

Chapter 4. Revelation

1. Milton Meltzer, *Dorothea Lange: A Photographer's Life* (Syracuse: N.Y. Syracuse University Press, 2000), p. 54.

2. Robert Coles, essay in *Dorothea Lange: Photographs of a Lifetime* (New York: Aperture Foundation, 1982), p. 12.

3. Ibid.

4. Suzanne Reiss, "Dorothea Lange: The Making of a Documentary Photographer," an interview with Dorothea Lange (1960–1961), Regional Oral History Office, University of California, Berkeley, 1968, p. 131.

5. Coles, p. 14.

6. Reiss interview, p. 136.

7. Ibid., p. 58.

8. Ibid., p. 139.

9. Ibid., p. 138.

10. Meltzer, p. 69.

Chapter 5. Beyond the Studio

1. Suzanne Reiss, "Dorothea Lange: The Making of a Documentary Photographer," an interview with Dorothea Lange (1960–1961), Regional Oral History Office, University of California, Berkeley, 1968, p. 149.

2. Pierre Borhan, *Dorothea Lange: The Heart and Mind of a Photographer* (Boston: Little, Brown and Company, 2002), p. 8.

3. Robert Coles, essay in *Dorothea Lange:*

Photographs of a Lifetime (New York: Aperture Foundation, 1982), p. 15.

4. Milton Meltzer, *Dorothea Lange: A Photographer's Life* (Syracuse, N.Y.: Syracuse University Press, 2000), p. 71.

5. Elizabeth Partridge, *Restless Spirit: The Life and Work of Dorothea Lange* (New York: Viking, 1998), pp. 42–43.

6. Coles essay, p. 15.

7. Suzanne Reiss, "Paul Schuster Taylor, California Social Scientist," an interview with Paul Taylor, Regional Oral History Office, University of California, Berkeley, 1973, p. 127.

8. Ibid., p. 136.

9. Ibid., p. 133.

10. Richard K. Doud, interview with Dorothea Lange, Archives of American Art, Smithsonian Institution, May 22, 1964, p. 8.

11. Reiss, Taylor interview, p. 128.

12. Ibid., pp. 129–130.

13. Doud interview, p. 7.

14. Reiss, Taylor interview, p. 133.

15. Meltzer, p. 97.

16. Partridge, p. 52.

17. Meltzer, p. 128.

Chapter 6. American Exodus

1. James N. Gregory, *American Exodus: The Dust Bowl Migration and Okie Culture in California* (Oxford: Oxford University Press, 1989), p. xiv.

2. Milton Meltzer, *Dorothea Lange: A Photographer's Life* (Syracuse, N.Y.: Syracuse University Press, 2000), p. 133.

3. Ibid.

4. Ibid.

5. Richard K. Doud, interview with Dorothea Lange, Archives of American Art, Smithsonian Institution, May 22, 1964, p. 8.

6. Suzanne Reiss, "Paul Schuster Taylor, California Social Scientist," an interview with Paul Taylor, Regional Oral History Office, University of California, Berkeley, 1973, p. 150.

7. Ibid., p. 152.

8. Ibid., p. 150.

9. Dorothea Lange and Paul Taylor, *An American Exodus: A Record of Human Erosion* (Paris: Jean-Michel Place, 1999), p. 5.

10. Ibid., p. 115.

11. Ibid., p. 14.

12. Meltzer, p. 203.

13. Ibid.

Chapter 7. The War Years

1. Milton Meltzer, *Dorothea Lange: A Photographer's Life* (Syracuse, N.Y.: Syracuse University Press, 2000), p. 208.

2. Ibid., p. 207.

3. Ibid., p. 233.

4. Suzanne Reiss, "Dorothea Lange: The Making of a Documentary Photographer," an interview with

Dorothea Lange (1960–1961), Regional Oral History Office, University of California, Berkeley, 1968, p. 190.

5. Ibid., pp. 187–188.

6. Meltzer, p. 242.

7. Charles Wollenberg, *Photographing the Second Gold Rush: Dorothea Lange and the East Bay at War, 1941-1945* (Berkeley, Calif.: Heyday Books, 1995), p. 14.

8. A.D. Coleman, *The New York Times*, September 24, 1972.

9. Wollenberg, p. 19.

10. Elizabeth Partridge, *Restless Spirit: The Life and Work of Dorothea Lange* (New York: Viking, 1998), p. 95.

11. Meltzer, p. 251.

12. Partridge, p. 97.

Chapter 8. Defining Photography

1. Karin Becker Ohrn, *Dorothea Lange and the Documentary Tradition* (Baton Rouge: Louisiana State University Press, 1980), p. 165.

2. Milton Meltzer, *Dorothea Lange: A Photographer's Life* (Syracuse, N.Y.: Syracuse University Press, 2000), p. 285.

3. Ibid., p. 286.

4. Ibid., p. 284.

5. Ohrn, p. 173.

6. Ibid., p. 174.

7. Ibid.

8. Meltzer, p. 152.

9. Ibid., p. 294.

10. Suzanne Reiss, "Dorothea Lange: The Making of a Documentary Photographer," an interview with Dorothea Lange (1960–1961), Regional Oral History Office, University of California, Berkeley, 1968, p. 211.

11. Aperture, 8:3 (1960).

12. Pierre Borhan, *Dorothea Lange: The Heart and Mind of a Photographer* (Boston: Little, Brown and Company, 2002), p. 254.

13. Meltzer, p. 306.

14. Ibid., p. 305.

Chapter 9. Retrospective

1. Elizabeth Partridge, *Restless Spirit: The Life and Work of Dorothea Lange* (New York: Viking, 1998), p. 101.

2. Milton Meltzer, *Dorothea Lange: A Photographer's Life* (Syracuse, N.Y.: Syracuse University Press, 2000), p. 320.

3. Ibid., p. 328.

4. Ibid., p. 318.

5. Karin Becker Ohrn, *Dorothea Lange and the Documentary Tradition* (Baton Rouge: Louisiana State University Press, 1980), p. 205.

6. Suzanne Reiss, "Dorothea Lange: The Making of a Documentary Photographer," an interview with Dorothea Lange (1960–1961), Regional Oral History Office, University of California, Berkeley, 1968, p. iii.

7. Ibid., p. 220.

8. Ohrn, pp. 203–204.

9. Suzanne Reiss, "Paul Schuster Taylor, California Social Scientist," an interview with Paul Taylor, Regional Oral History Office, University of California, Berkeley, 1973, p. 284.

10. Ohrn, p. 220.

11. Dorothea Lange in conversation with John Szarkowski, recorded in the documentary *Under the Trees.*

12. Ohrn, p. 225.

13. Robert Coles, essay in *Dorothea Lange: Photographs of a Lifetime* (New York: Aperture Foundation, 1982), p. 39.

14. Pierre Borhan, *Dorothea Lange: The Heart and Mind of a Photographer* (Boston: Little, Brown and Company, 2002), p. 256.

15. Reiss, "Dorothea Lange," p. 252.

Chapter 10. Enduring Record

1. Suzanne Reiss, "Dorothea Lange: The Making of a Documentary Photographer," an interview with Dorothea Lange (1960–1961), Regional Oral History Office, University of California, Berkeley, 1968, pp. 175–176.

2. Ibid., Appendix, p. 250.

3. Ibid., Appendix, p. 247.

4. Dorothea Lange, photographs with text in *Dorothea Lange: Photographs of a Lifetime* (New York: Aperture Foundation, 1982), p. 46.

5. Reiss, "Dorothea Lange," p. 214.

6. Ibid.

7. Suzanne Reiss, "Paul Schuster Taylor, California Social Scientist," an interview with Paul Taylor, Regional Oral History Office, University of California, Berkeley, 1973, p. 298.

8. Robert Coles, essay in *Dorothea Lange: Photographs of a Lifetime* (New York: Aperture Foundation, 1982), p. 20.

9. Elizabeth Partridge, *Restless Spirit: The Life and Work of Dorothea Lange* (New York: Viking, 1998), p. 57.

10. Reiss, "Dorothea Lange," Appendix, p. 240.

11. Ibid., p. 174.

12. Pierre Borhan, *Dorothea Lange: The Heart and Mind of a Photographer* (Boston: Little, Brown and Company, 2002), p. 59.

13. Coles essay, p. 124.

14. Ibid., p. 152.

15. Ibid., p. 7.

FURTHER READING

Acker, Kerry. *Dorothea Lange.* Broomall, Pa.: Chelsea House, 2004.

Gaines, Ann Graham. *American Photographers: Capturing the Image.* Berkeley Heights, N.J.: Enslow Publishers, Inc., 2002.

Partridge, Elizabeth. *Restless Spirit: The Life and Work of Dorothea Lange.* New York: Viking, 2001.

Sills, Leslie. *In Real Life: Six Women Photographers.* New York: Holiday House, 2002.

Turner, Robyn Montana. *Dorothea Lange.* Boston: Little, Brown and Company, 1994.

INTERNET ADDRESSES

Oakland Museum of California
http://museumofcalifornia.org/global/art/
    collections_dorothea_lange.html

Library of Congress Exhibition

*Women Come to the Front: Journalists, Photographers,
and Broadcasters During World War II*

http://www.loc.gov/exhibits/wcf/wcf0013.html

The History Place
http://www.historyplace.com/unitedstates/lange/
    index.html

INDEX